DRAG RACERS

by Jeffrey Zuehlke

Nick Licata, consultant, drag racing photographer

Lerner Publications Company • Minneapolis

For Graham Zuehlke, fastest in the quarter mile

Cover Photo: Hillary Will races in a National Hotrod Racing Association Top Fuel event in Reading, Pennsylvania.

Lerner Publications Company
A division of Lerner Publishing Group, Inc.
241 First Avenue North
Minneapolis, MN 55401 U.S.A.

Website address: www.lernerbooks.com

Library of Congress Cataloging-in-Publication Data

Zuehlke, Jeffrey, 1968-
    Drag racers / by Jeffrey Zuehlke.
        p.   cm. — (Motor mania)
    Includes bibliographical references and index.
    ISBN 978–0–8225–7287–9 (lib. bdg. : alk. paper)
    1. Dragsters—Juvenile literature. 2. Drag racers—Juvenile literature. I. Title.
TL236.2.Z84 2008
    796.72—dc22   2007010116

Manufactured in the United States of America
1 2 3 4 5 6 – DP – 13 12 11 10 09 08

Contents

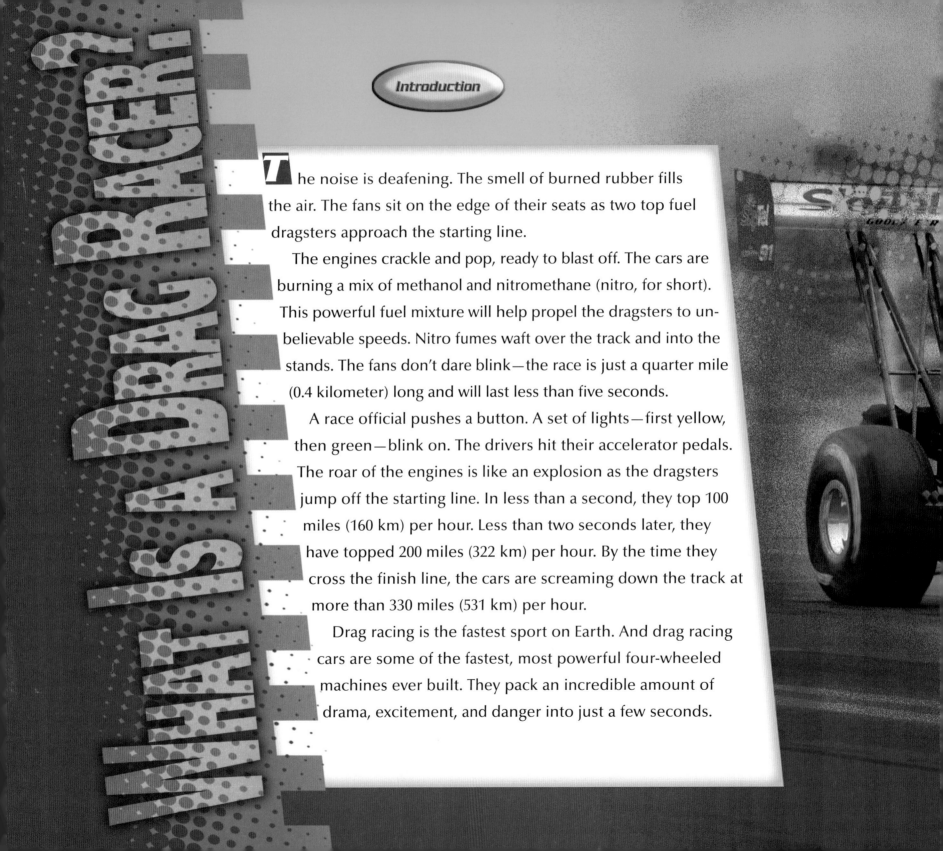

Introduction

The noise is deafening. The smell of burned rubber fills the air. The fans sit on the edge of their seats as two top fuel dragsters approach the starting line.

The engines crackle and pop, ready to blast off. The cars are burning a mix of methanol and nitromethane (nitro, for short). This powerful fuel mixture will help propel the dragsters to un-believable speeds. Nitro fumes waft over the track and into the stands. The fans don't dare blink—the race is just a quarter mile (0.4 kilometer) long and will last less than five seconds.

A race official pushes a button. A set of lights—first yellow, then green—blink on. The drivers hit their accelerator pedals. The roar of the engines is like an explosion as the dragsters jump off the starting line. In less than a second, they top 100 miles (160 km) per hour. Less than two seconds later, they have topped 200 miles (322 km) per hour. By the time they cross the finish line, the cars are screaming down the track at more than 330 miles (531 km) per hour.

Drag racing is the fastest sport on Earth. And drag racing cars are some of the fastest, most powerful four-wheeled machines ever built. They pack an incredible amount of drama, excitement, and danger into just a few seconds.

Headers (exhaust pipes) belch flames as Larry Dixon's top fuel dragster pounces off the starting line.

Top Fuel, Funny Car, Pro Stock Car, Pro Stock Bike

Drag racing is a large and diverse sport. Both amateurs and professionals compete in many different cars and classes. This book will focus on the four professional classes that compete in the National Hot Rod Association's (NHRA) POWERade Drag Racing Series. They are top fuel, funny car, pro stock car, and pro stock bike.

Top fuel dragsters *(left)* are the fastest and most powerful drag racers. These machines are long and thin. They have massive rear tires and small, bicycle-sized front wheels. A top fueler's engine is near the back of the car, behind the driver. A large wing, called an airfoil, is mounted high above and behind the rear wheel. The airfoil works like an upside-down wing, pushing the rear tires onto the track. A smaller wing at the front keeps the front wheels on the ground.

Funny cars *(right)* are nearly as fast as dragsters. Funny cars have a more traditional car shape but are much longer than road cars. The engine is mounted in the center of the funny car, in front of the driver. Like dragsters, they have huge rear tires and small front wheels.

Pro stock cars *(left)* are the same size and shape as road cars. The term *stock* means "straight from the factory." But these machines are heavily modified (changed) for racing. With thick rear tires, a large hood scoop to send air into the engine, and a rear wing (known as a spoiler), these machines can go more than 200 miles (320 km) per hour.

Pro stock bikes *(right)* are among the world's fastest motorcycles. Equipped with large, powerful engines and fat rear tires, a pro stock bike can top 180 miles (290 km) per hour in a quarter-mile (0.4 km) run.

Chapter One

DRAG RACING HISTORY

Drag Racing: The Beginning

No one is quite sure where the term *drag race* came from. But we do know that in the late 1940s, a whole generation of young people were involved in a pastime called hot rodding. Hot-rodders modified their regular cars to make them faster. They called their "souped-up" cars hot rods.

And what do you do with a souped-up hot rod? Why, race it, of course! Racing was fun but dangerous. And because of the danger, it was illegal to race on the streets.

But not even the long arm of the law could stop people from getting their speed buzz. So the solution was

A hot-rodder poses with his hot rod outside Sacramento, California, in the late 1940s.

to find a way to make racing legal and safer. The way to do this was to set up a controlled racing environment.

The First Drag Race

In April 1949, a group of hot-rodders got together on a lonely stretch of road near Santa Barbara, California. For several hours, dozens of hot-rodders enjoyed some racing. The cars raced in pairs—two cars, side by side.

So what made this event different from street races? It was legal. The hot-rodders had gotten permission to race from the California Highway Patrol. The patrol had allowed them to close off the road from traffic. Many people say this gathering was the first true drag racing event. Soon after, similar racing meets began to take place around the country.

Wally Parks and the NHRA

In 1951 a Californian named Wally Parks founded the National Hot Rod Association (NHRA). Parks was a salesman and hot-rodder. He saw a

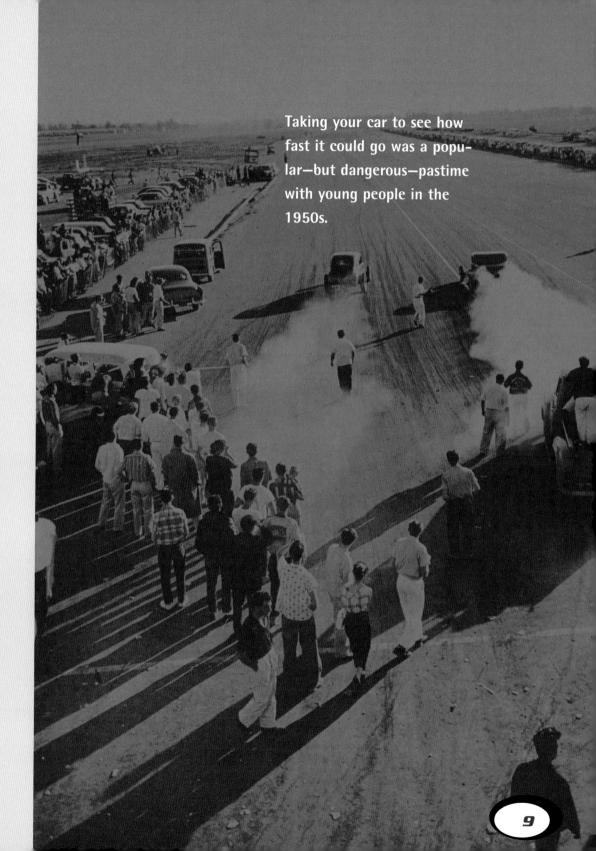

Taking your car to see how fast it could go was a popular—but dangerous—pastime with young people in the 1950s.

big future for hot rodding and drag racing. The NHRA laid out rules and guidelines for drag racing. It also organized events and helped promote safer racing. The NHRA worked with law enforcement agencies to get permission to hold events.

Parks's group set up its first race in 1953. Within a few years, it was organizing races around the country. A new and exciting sport was gathering speed. In 1955 the NHRA organized the first national championship in Great Bend, Kansas. A yearly tradition was born.

Meanwhile, clever hot-rodders were finding new ways to go faster.

Some used special fuels. The most popular fuel was nitromethane. Nitro is a chemical used in paint thinner— and in rocket fuel. The stuff is powerful and dangerous. It can explode if handled improperly. But it can jack up horsepower (hp) like nothing else. An engine that normally produced 200 hp could get up to 300 hp by burning nitro (if it didn't blow up entirely).

At the same time, a few ambitious racers were building cars just for the drag strip. These dragsters were lighter, stronger, and faster than plain old souped-up cars. Every hot-rodder had a different idea for how to go faster. No

Comparing Horsepower

Horsepower is the unit used to measure an engine's power. The following comparisons give a good idea of the mind-blowing power of a top fuel dragster engine.

Lawn mower	6 hp
Mazda MX5 (small sports car)	150 hp
Heavy-duty pickup truck	400 hp
NASCAR stock car engine	850 hp
Top fuel dragster	8,000 hp

two cars looked quite the same. Some were long, and some were short. Some had more than one engine. A few even had four! Other hot-rodders worked to make their cars as light as possible.

These changes made the cars faster. In turn, the faster cars made the racing more exciting. More and more people showed up to watch. Across the country, people were building drag strips. These were places spe-cially designed for drag racing. They featured a quarter mile (0.4 km) strip, grandstands for spectators, and pit areas where mechanics could work.

By the end of the 1950s, drag racing was becoming more than just a pas-time. For a few people, it was a profes-sional sport. Drivers such as "Big Daddy" Don Garlits, "TV Tommy" Ivo, and Art Chrisman drew big crowds wherever they raced.

The Bug was built in the 1950s by drag racer Dick Kraft. Kraft took to the extreme the idea that less weight equals more speed. He stripped an old car down to the frame and dropped a big engine into it. The car was fast, ugly—and very unsafe.

Slingshots

The drivers weren't the only stars of the show. The cars kept getting more and more sophisticated. They were also getting a whole lot faster.

By the 1960s, a basic dragster design was taking shape. It started with a frame, or chassis, made of strong metal tubing. The suspension (the parts that connect the wheels to the car) was attached to the chassis. The engine was mounted just in front of the large rear wheels. The cockpit (driver compartment) was located behind the rear wheels. The driver sat at the very back, looking a bit like a ball in a slingshot. So people nicknamed this style of dragster a slingshot.

Racers worked to perfect the slingshot design throughout the 1960s. They made the cars slimmer, with needle-shaped front ends. They also set the cars lower. The bottom of the chassis rode just inches off the ground. The slimmer, lower shape made the dragsters very aerodynamic—they cut through the air more easily. Speeds kept climbing. In 1964 Garlits made the first 200-mile-per-hour (320 km) run in his slingshot.

Slingshots got their name from the way the driver's head looked like a ball in a slingshot, ready to launch. They also seemed to accelerate nearly as fast as a ball launched from a slingshot. This is a double-engined dragster.

Funny Cars

Dragsters ruled the raceways in the early 1960s. They were the stars of the show. But as the decade went on, a new kind of racer began to steal some of the spotlight—funny cars.

By the 1960s, U.S. automakers Chrysler (which produced Chrysler, Dodge, and Plymouth cars), Ford (Ford, Mercury, and other cars), and General Motors (Chevrolet, Pontiac, and others) had become involved in drag racing. These companies realized that success on the track would mean better sales for all of their cars. So they supplied cars for a handful of top racers.

But these cars were not dragsters. The automakers wanted to showcase machines that *looked* like the same cars they sold for the street. So they supplied models of their most popular cars for the super stock and A/FX classes (A/FX stands for altered/factory experimental). These two classes were similar to today's pro stock class. Soon enough,

engineers started coming up with ways to make these "stock" cars faster.

In 1965, Chrysler's engineers introduced cars with altered wheelbases. The wheelbase is the distance between a car's front and rear axles. (An axle is a metal bar to which the wheel is attached). Chrysler's engineers had figured out that moving the wheels forward on the chassis gave the cars better traction. Their look was unusual. People started calling them funny cars.

The A/FX class—such as the Dodge above—was created so manufacturers could show off their products on the drag strip. These machines would later evolve into funny cars.

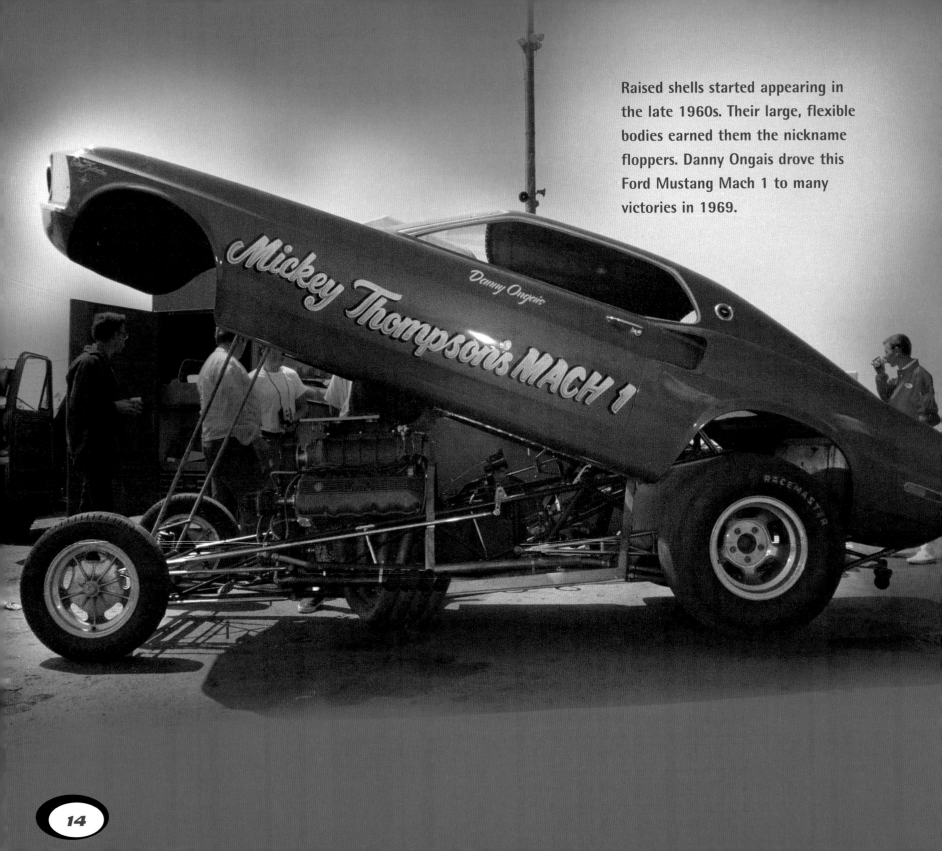

Raised shells started appearing in the late 1960s. Their large, flexible bodies earned them the nickname floppers. Danny Ongais drove this Ford Mustang Mach 1 to many victories in 1969.

But that wasn't the only change. The engineers enlarged the rear wheel wells so they could fit extra large rear tires in them. (Big rear tires gave the cars better grip for fast starts.) Engineers also replaced some metal parts with fiberglass to make the cars lighter.

In 1966 Mercury hired a chassis-building company to create a whole new chassis for its Comet racer. The result was a tube frame chassis similar to a dragster's.

Faster and Funnier

Mercury also hired a company to create a fiberglass body shell. The one-piece shell was attached to the rear of the chassis with a hinge. The whole shell could be raised or lowered like a car's hood. With the body lowered, the funny car looked like a normal car with an altered wheelbase. But it was much lighter. And much, much faster. The new Mercury tore up the drag strips, breaking many class records.

Mercury's competitors copied the design. This new class of drag racing—funny car—was quickly gaining in popularity.

Drivers worked to get more speed from their funny cars. They added bigger engines and superchargers. These devices had been used on dragsters for years. Superchargers, or blowers, force more air and fuel into the engine. They provide a big boost in power. To top it off, more of the racers started using nitro. Within a few years, funny cars were starting to catch up to dragsters in speeds and elapsed times.

The fans loved funny cars. There was something exciting about seeing machines that looked like regular cars driving at 200 miles (320 km) per hour. And funny car races could be very exciting and unpredictable. The floppers, as funny cars were sometimes called, were tougher to drive than dragsters. They tended to shake and wobble when they got out of control. Fans loved the show.

DID YOU KNOW?
Every drag racing run is measured in two ways. Elapsed time (e.t.) is the most important measurement. It is the amount of time a car takes to go from start to finish. Miles (or kilometers) per hour is the speed the car is going when it crosses the finish line.

That Thing Got a Hemi?

A V8 is an engine with eight cylinders arranged in the shape of a V. All top fuel and funny cars use custom-built V8 engines with "hemi," or hemispherical (half-globe-shaped), combustion chambers. Like engines on road cars, these machines create power through combustion.

They burn a mixture of air and fuel—nitromethane and methanol. The air and fuel mixture is injected into the combustion chamber. The upward movement of the piston presses together the air and fuel mixture. Then a spark plug ignites (sets fire) to the mixture. The explosion pushes the piston downward, creating power.

Hemi Cylinder

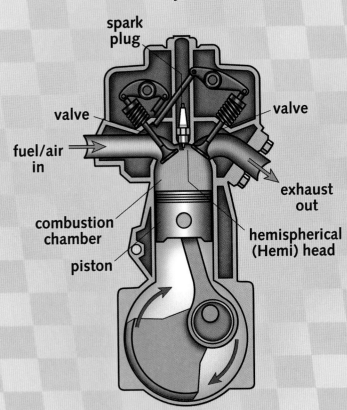

spark plug

valve

valve

fuel/air in

exhaust out

combustion chamber

hemispherical (Hemi) head

piston

A Hemi engine mounted to a dragster

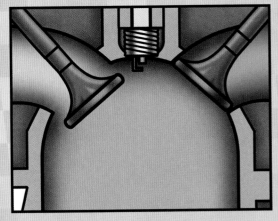

Close-up view of a Hemi's combustion chamber with its rounded (Hemi) top surface

Don Garlits's *(right)* Swamp Rat
XIV (below) showed that a
rear-engine car could beat the
slingshots.

Rear-Engine Revolution

Drag racing engineers were always looking for new ways to make their cars faster. Safety, however, wasn't always as important as having the fastest car on the strip. But the top fuel class went through a big change in the early 1970s. In March 1970, Don Garlits suffered serious injuries when his slingshot's gearbox exploded. The engine and gearbox sat within a few inches of his legs and feet. The explosion injured both of his legs and blew off part of his foot. Garlits decided he would not drive a front-engine dragster again. Instead, he designed and built a new kind of machine. This one had the engine behind the driver. Engine and gearbox explosions would take place behind the driver.

Other drivers had tried this design before. But the cars were never as fast as the front-engine slingshots. Don Garlits wasn't your average racer, though. The Floridian is one of the greatest minds in motor sports history. He made the design for his *Swamp Rat XIV* car work—big time.

He won the first race of the 1971 NHRA season and kept on winning. His design had better balance than a front-engine dragster. The car was easier to drive. And without a giant, roaring engine in the front, the driver could see better.

Soon Garlits added a big wing to the back of his car. (Racers had already been experimenting with wings in front.) This airfoil worked like an upside-down airplane wing. It created downforce. When air rushed over it, it pushed the back of the car down. The downforce gave the car better traction and better stability.

Garlits ruled the raceways in 1971. So of course, his rivals began to copy the rear-engine design. Within a few years, the slingshot was a thing of the past.

Meanwhile, speeds kept climbing and elapsed times kept dropping. In 1975 Garlits broke the 250-miles-per-hour (402 km) mark in his *Swamp Rat XXII*. That record also made him the

Garlits *(top)* beats a rival off the starting line. Note how Garlits's rear tires are wrinkling as they grip the track. The other car's tires are smoking—a sign of wheelspin.

first to break the five-second elapsed time barrier. He had covered the quarter-mile (0.4 km) strip in an amazing 5.63 seconds.

Funny Cars, Big Stars

The sport of drag racing grew fast throughout the 1970s. Events were shown on television, giving millions of people the chance to enjoy the excitement. Big-money corporations signed sponsorship deals with the NHRA and with racing teams. The sponsors helped pay for the cars and equipment. In return, the teams put the sponsors' names and logos on the cars and on signs around the track.

A big rivalry in the funny car class added to the interest. Don "Snake" Prudhomme was one of funny car's top stars. In the 1970s, he shared a friendly rivalry with Tom McEwen. McEwen picked up the nickname Mongoose. (A mongoose is an animal that hunts and kills snakes.) The Snake and Mongoose drew huge crowds

wherever they raced. And they sold a lot of toys for their sponsor, Mattel, the maker of Hot Wheels cars.

The NHRA featured many star drivers in the 1970s and 1980s. Bob Glidden ruled the pro stock class, winning 10 titles. In 1977 top fuel driver Shirley Muldowney became the first female NHRA champion. In the funny car

Don "Snake" Prudhomme's legendary U.S. Army–sponsored funny car was one of the most famous race cars of the 1970s.

class, Don Schumacher, "Jungle Jim" Liberman, Raymond Beadle, and Ed "the Ace" McCulloch all earned fame during these years. And funny car's biggest star, Kenny Bernstein, won four funny car titles in the 1980s.

Meanwhile, the sport's best mechanical minds kept finding ways to get more speed out of the cars. Funny car teams used wind tunnels to test aerodynamic body shapes. The teams tried out new shapes that could cut through the air as fast as possible. In time, funny cars looked less and less like road cars. The newest floppers are far longer and lower than anything you might see on the street.

The basic top fuel design hasn't changed much over the years. Garlits's rear-engine layout is still in use. But recent dragsters are longer than they were in the past. The newest top fuelers have a whopping 300-inch (762-centimeter) wheelbase. By comparison, Garlits's *Swamp Rat XXII* had a 250-inch (635 cm) wheelbase.

In 1990 Bernstein switched from funny cars to top fuel. Two years later, he became the first driver to run 300 miles (483 km) per hour. Four years after that, he won a top fuel title. No other driver had won the crown in different classes before. During those days, Bernstein's biggest rival was another legend, Joe Amato. But none of these

Not Just for Boys

For the most part, men have dominated motor sports. Women have had few opportunities. But this is not the case in drag racing. One of the greatest top fuel drivers in history is a woman—Shirley Muldowney. Her success helped pave the way for many other women, including Angelle Sampey *(below)* (a multiple pro stock bike champion), Melanie Troxel (top fuel), Hillary Will (top fuel), and Erica Enders (pro stock).

Faster, Faster, Faster!

Here's a list of major top fuel speed records and the drivers who broke them:

- **200 miles (322 km) per hour:**
  Don Garlits, 1964
- **250 miles (402 km) per hour:**
  Don Garlits, 1975
- **300 miles (483 km) per hour:**
  Kenny Bernstein, 1992
- **330 miles (531 km) per hour:**
  Tony Schumacher, 1999

racers matched the success of the man who ruled the 1990s—John Force.

New Faces

John Force is the most successful driver in drag racing history. He has won more events and more championships than anyone else. After years of trying and failing, he won his first funny car championship in 1990. He followed that up with another one in 1991. He finished second in 1992 before pulling off an unbelievable run.

Force went on to win the next 10 funny car titles. No athlete, driver, or team in any major sport has ever won so many titles in a row.

Along the way, the excitable Force has become the sport's biggest star. And he keeps on winning. In 2006 Force took his record 14th funny car title. The following year, his daughter Ashley joined funny car's top ranks. She has already become one of the sport's most popular drivers.

In top fuel, Tony Schumacher has been the man to beat in the 2000s. But the four-time title winner has plenty of competition from Doug Kalitta, Brandon Bernstein, Larry Dixon, and others. In recent years, a new group of talented racers has come along as well. They include Melanie Troxel and J. R. Todd. In 2006 the young Todd became the first African American to win a top fuel event. With so much talent and star power, drag racing has a bright and exciting future ahead.

J. R. Todd is the first African American to win a top fuel event. Still in his early twenties, he is one of the sport's most popular young drivers.

Chapter Two

Drag Racing Culture

After more than 50 years of thrills, drag racing continues to be one of the world's most exciting sports. Its loyal fans watch the action on TV and come out to the raceways in huge numbers each year.

Drag racing is a fan-friendly sport. On race days, spectators can wander through the pit areas. They can watch the teams work on the cars and get a whiff of those powerful nitro fumes. If they show up at the right time, fans might even be able to get autographs from their favorite drivers. Few other sports give spectators a chance to get so close to the action.

The Season

The NHRA POWERade Drag Racing Series begins every February. The top

fuel, funny car, and pro stock competitions kick off with the Winternationals event at Auto Club Raceway in Pomona, California. (The pro stock bike season begins about a month later.) From then, events are held about every other weekend.

The POWERade season includes 23 events. In late October or early November, the excitement finishes where it started—in Pomona at the NHRA Finals. In between, the racers visit every corner of the country and many places in between—from New Jersey to Florida to Washington State.

At every event, drivers and teams earn points toward the championship. Drivers earn points by qualifying for races, winning elimination rounds, winning events, and setting elapsed time records.

For years the points system was

Two top fuel dragsters prepare to race at the biggest event of the year—the five-day U.S. Nationals at Indianapolis Raceway Park in Indianapolis, Indiana.

simple. The driver and team that earned the most points won the championship. But the system had some flaws. A driver could build up a huge points lead. It was possible to clinch the title with several races still left in the season. Without the championship at stake, those late races lost some drama.

So in 2007, the NHRA added a new wrinkle to the competition—the Countdown to the Championship. For the first 17 races, teams in each class compete for points as usual. After that, the eight teams with the most points face off in a six-race, playoff-style countdown. The Countdown starts at the biggest event of the year, the U.S. Nationals at Indianapolis Raceway Park in Indianapolis, Indiana. From there, the eight top teams battle it out. The season ends in Pomona with the top two teams competing for the title.

A Race Weekend

Drag racing is a big business. Teams spend millions of dollars on equipment,

Qualifying Results

Competitors earn 10 points for making a qualifying run, even if they don't make the top 16. Those who do qualify earn bonus points on top of the 10 points. Bonus points are added according to qualifying position.

First (top qualifier): 8 points
Second: 7 points
Third: 6 points
Fourth: 5 points
Fifth and sixth: 4 points
Seventh and eighth: 3 points
Ninth through 12th: 2 points
13th through 16th: 1 point

The NHRA also awards 20 bonus points for setting an official elapsed time record.

including the custom-built semitrailers that carry the cars. The top teams also have large motor homes that they use for working and living spaces.

NHRA POWERade series events last from three to six days. The teams usually arrive at the track on a Wednesday or Thursday. They unload the cars, tools, and equipment. Then they get ready for the first races, which start on Friday.

The racing starts with qualifying. For a three-day event, the professional teams start making qualifying runs on Friday. Each car makes four runs, two on Friday and two on Saturday. On most runs, two cars race side by side. But they are not actually racing each other. Instead, they are racing the clock. The goal in qualifying is to clock one of the 16 fastest times. In each class, between 20 and 30 drivers will try to qualify. But only the fastest 16 in each class will make "the show"—the Sunday shootout for the win. The rest will pack up their trailers and head home.

Sunday is the big event—eliminations. The 16 qualifiers in each class face off in a tournament. In the first round, the car with the fastest qualifying time faces the car with the 16th-fastest time. The second-fastest car faces the 15th-fastest car, and so on. The winner of each run moves on to the next. The loser is eliminated. He or she goes home.

A crowd of drag racing fans gather as Tony Schumacher's top fuel dragster is removed from its trailer. Another action-packed weekend is about to begin.

When darkness falls, the nitro-burning cars light up the night.

limit. The results can be spectacular—and dangerous. Crashes do happen, although serious injuries are rare.

Each class has four elimination rounds. After each round, the field is cut in half. The number of racers goes from 16 to 8 to 4 to 2. The top two cars face off in the final round.

The winner of the final round is named top eliminator and receives a trophy, a big cash prize, and 100 series points. The runner-up gets 80 points—and probably a bad taste in his or her mouth from coming so close but losing. After the final race, the teams

With each elimination, the excitement builds. One tiny mistake by a driver can cost a precious split second and ruin a run. Things that can go wrong include spinning the tires, letting the car wiggle out of "the groove," or blowing an engine. A 4.5-second run doesn't leave much room for error! The cars are pushed to the limit. It doesn't take much to go over that

Drag Racing Term

The groove: on every run, the driver tries to keep the car in "the groove." This is the part of the track where the car runs most comfortably. Over a race weekend, the cars burn more and more rubber from their tires onto the groove. The car tires stick better to the rubbery surface.

pack up their trailers and begin to get ready for the next event.

Going for a Run

Every drag racing run starts with a burnout. A section near the start of the track is wetted down with water. The driver spins the rear tires in the water. This cleans the tires and heats them up for better grip. Burnouts also create a big cloud of white smoke. They are one of the most exciting parts of every run.

After doing their burnouts, the two cars back up behind the starting line.

Then they slowly move forward. As they roll ahead, the drivers keep their eyes on the "Christmas tree." This is a tower with sets of amber (yellow), green, and red lights.

When one of the cars gets within about 6 or 8 inches (15 or 20 cm) of the starting line, it sets off the first group of amber lights at the top of the tree. This signals that the car is "pre-staged." It is nearly at the starting line.

From there, the driver slowly inches forward. When the car's tires reach the starting line, the second set of

Tire smoke fills the air as Cory McClenathan does a full-blown burnout.

NHRA starter Rick Stewart

amber lights goes on. This means the car is "staged." It is ready to race.

Once both cars are staged, the race is ready to begin. The event is now in the hands of a race official—the "starter." (Rick Stewart is the starter at all NHRA national events.) He pushes a button. Three sets of amber lights flash. Exactly four-tenths of a second later, the green light goes on, and the race begins.

Drivers try to time their starts so the cars jump off the line right when the green lights go on. How well drivers do this is called their reaction time. If a driver starts too soon, the red light goes on. This means the driver has fouled. He or she is disqualified and is out of the race.

Once the race begins, the driver has to have just the right touch. Too much power can make the tires spin, costing valuable time. Too little power results in a slow start—and usually a loss.

With the car roaring down the strip, the driver needs to keep the car's tires in the groove. Controlling 8,000 hp is difficult! If the engine loses power in one or more cylinders, it can push the car sideways. The driver needs to hang on and keep going straight. The car cannot cross the centerline that divides the track. Crossing the centerline results in disqualification.

The driver can't turn sharply. The turns must be smooth. A sharp turn at 300 miles (483 km) per hour will send the car out of control.

If the tires start to shake or slip, the

Seventy-Five-Minute Rush

Between runs, the pit crew strips down the car *(left)*. They inspect every part for damage. Then they put the whole machine back together. The driver hops in and cranks the engine to see how it runs. If everything goes according to plan, the car goes back out to the track for the next run. The crew has only 75 minutes to complete this process.

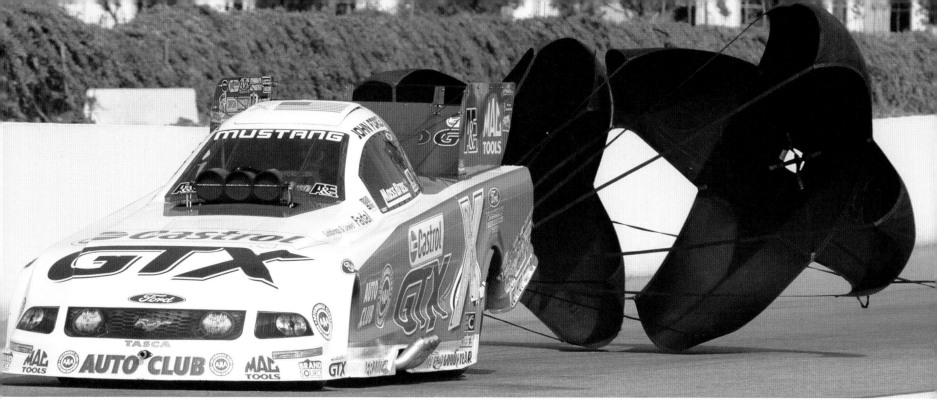

driver needs to ease off the accelerator pedal to get the tires to grip the surface again. Sometimes the car just won't grip. So the driver needs to "pedal" the car—push and let up on the accelerator repeatedly—to the finish line.

If all goes well, the car screams down the track. It crosses the finish line. A timer records the elapsed time and the winner. Another device records the speed at which the car was traveling.

The driver "pops the chutes" and pulls the brake handle. A pair of parachutes open from the rear of the car.

The chutes and brakes slow down the speeding vehicle.

The driver glides the car into the shutdown area. He or she gets out and celebrates a win—or agonizes over a loss. Then the car is towed back to the pit area to prepare for the next run.

Drag Racing Term

Pedalfest: a run in which both drivers have to pedal their cars to the finish line

A pair of parachutes opens to slow down John Force's funny car.

As "the tree" goes green, every fraction of a second counts. Here the rear tires of Bruce Litton's dragster wrinkle as they grip the track.

Safety

Drag racing can be a dangerous sport. Over the years, hundreds of drivers have lost their lives in racing accidents. In the old hot-rodding days, drivers didn't do much to protect themselves. Many hot-rodders raced in jeans and short-sleeve shirts. Few even had—or used—seat belts!

Modern drag racers are designed to be as safe as possible. The chassis are made of strong tubing. Top fuel dragsters, funny cars, and pro stock cars all have roll cages. These are ultrastrong structures that protect the driver during crashes.

Funny cars have hatches on their roofs. They allow the driver to hop out of the car if it catches fire. Some funny cars also have hatches on the side windows. They allow the driver to escape out of the side, if the car flips onto its roof. Funny cars and pro stock cars also have fire extinguishers inside them.

Drivers wear seat belts, of course. In fact, they wear a five-point harness that keeps them strapped in tight. Drivers also wear special clothing that protects them from fire. These fire suits are made of layers of special fire-resistant fabric.

The top hatch allows funny car drivers to get out fast.

Multiple top fuel champion Tony Schumacher strapped into his U.S. Army dragster

Top fuel driver Brandon Bernstein wearing the HANS device. The system of collar and straps keeps the driver's head stable in the event of a crash.

A shatterproof helmet protects the driver's head. Drivers also wear a head and neck support (HANS) device. HANS is a collar and set of straps. The straps are connected to the driver's helmet. HANS keeps the driver's head and neck from snapping violently in a crash.

Yet despite these many safety features, drag racing will always be a dangerous sport. This was proven again in March 2007, when funny car driver Eric Medlen died from injuries he suffered during a test session at Gainesville Raceway in Florida. Medlen's death was a grim reminder of the dangers of drag racing. Yet the NHRA remains committed to safety. The organization is always working to keep the world's fastest sport as exciting and safe as possible.

Drag Racing on TV

The ESPN2 cable network covers all NHRA national events. Check your local listings, or visit ESPN's website: http://espn.com

IHRA events are shown on the SPEED cable network. Visit http://www.speedtv.com.

Something for Everyone

You don't need to be a professional driver to go drag racing. In fact, most drag racers are amateurs—they do it just for fun. The NHRA calls its classes for amateurs "sportsman classes."

The NHRA approves more than 200 sportsman classes. They include top alcohol dragsters, as well as comp, super stock, and super street. A top alcohol dragster looks much like a top fueler. But a top alcohol dragster runs just on methanol. Comp (short for competition) classes cover a variety of gasoline-burning cars. Super stock cars look much like stock vehicles. Cars in the super street class look almost like regular cars.

POWERade Drag Racing Series Tour Tracks

CANADA

Seattle, Washington

Brainerd, Minnesota

Chicago, Illinois

Norwalk, Ohio

Englishtown, New Jersey

Reading, Pennsylvania

Sonoma, California

Denver, Colorado

Topeka, Kansas

Indianapolis, Indiana

Richmond, Virginia

Las Vegas, Nevada

UNITED STATES

Madison, Illinois

Pomona, California

Bristol, Tennessee

Phoenix, Arizona

Memphis, Tennessee

Atlanta, Georgia

Dallas, Texas

Houston, Texas

Gainesville, Florida

MEXICO

Joe Amato (born 1944)

The Pennsylvania native is the most successful driver in NHRA top fuel history, with a record 52 event wins. He is the first top fuel driver to win five championships and may have won more if eye problems hadn't led to his retirement in 2000.

Seasons: 1982–2000

National Event Wins: 52

NHRA Championships: 5 (top fuel: 1984, 1988, 1990–1992)

Kenny Bernstein (born 1944)

The six-time champion is called the King of Speed. In 1992 the New Mexico native became the first to run 300 miles (483 km) per hour. He is one of just two drivers to win NHRA championships in both funny car and top fuel. Bernstein is also one of motor sports' smartest businessmen. At one time, he owned a drag racing team, a NASCAR stock car team, and an IndyCar® team. In 2007 he came out of retirement to race funny cars. His son Brandon is also a successful top fuel driver.

Seasons: 1972–1973, 1978–2002, 2007–

National Event Wins: 60

NHRA Championships: 6 (funny car: 1985–1988; top fuel: 1996, 2001)

Joe Amato's top fuel dragster

Kenny Bernstein's 2000s-era top fuel dragster

John Force (born 1949)

Force isn't just drag racing's greatest winner—he might be the greatest winner in all of sports. His 10 straight NHRA funny car championships (1993–2002) is the greatest run of success ever seen in a major professional sport. Only the Boston Celtics, who won eight straight National Basketball Association titles, have come close. Force's dominance on the track is matched by his dominance in front of the microphone. His high-energy personality has made him a fan favorite and drag racing's biggest star.

Seasons: 1978–

National Event Wins: 122

NHRA Championships: 14 (funny car: 1990, 1991, 1993–2002, 2004, 2006)

Don Garlits (born 1932)

Most fans consider Big Daddy to be the greatest drag racing driver of all time. Garlits won 17 titles in NHRA, IHRA, and AHRA competition. Yet his incredible driving career is only part of the Garlits legend. He was also one of the sport's greatest innovators. His Swamp Rat series of cars were always among the best on the track. And his revolutionary rear-engine top fuel car design led to faster run times and probably saved some lives in the process.

Seasons: 1955–1992

National Event Wins: 144 (including NHRA, IHRA, and AHRA)

NHRA Championships: 6 (NHRA U.S. Nationals championships: 1964, 1967, 1968; NHRA points titles: 1975, 1985, 1986)

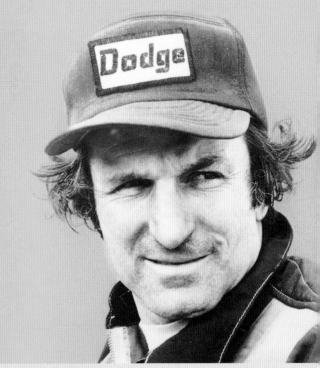

John Force's 2007
Castrol GTX funny car

Don Garlits's *Swamp Rat XXI*

Bob Glidden (born 1944)

Glidden is one of the greatest pro stock drivers in NHRA history. No other pro stocker even comes close to his 10 NHRA championships. His 85 NHRA national event wins was a record for many years until John Force broke it in 2000. An Indiana native, Glidden began his pro stock career in 1972 and won his first championship a year later. He went on to dominate his class through the 1970s and much of the 1980s, setting numerous pro stock records along the way.

Seasons: 1972–1997

National Event Wins: 85

NHRA Championships: 10 (pro stock: 1974, 1975, 1978–1980, 1985–1989)

Tommy Ivo (born 1936)

TV Tommy was one of drag racing's first big stars. But he earned his fame before he ever set foot in a dragster. As a youngster, Ivo appeared in nearly 100 movies and 200 television programs. His success as an actor earned him the money to follow his dream—racing. His wealth allowed him to invest in the best equipment possible, including the first twin-engine dragster. But this star of the 1950s and 1960s wasn't just a rich pretty boy. He was a smart mechanic and a very fast driver. Ivo was the first drag racer to break 170 miles (274 km) per hour and then 180 miles (290 km) per hour.

Seasons: 1959–1982

National Event Wins: 1

NHRA Championships: 0

Bob Glidden's car

One of Tommy Ivo's 1960s
multiple-engine slingshot dragsters

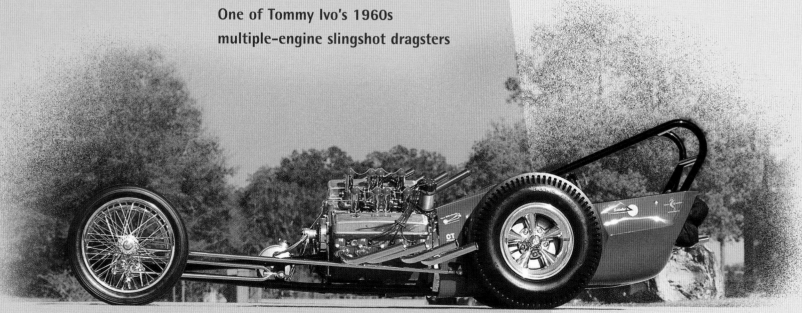

Warren Johnson (born 1943)

This Minnesota native is one of the most successful pro stock drivers of all time. Only the great Bob Glidden comes close to Johnson's 96 national event wins, 6 NHRA titles, and 2 IHRA titles. But Johnson's talents go beyond the driver's seat. He is also a brilliant mechanic and engineer and one of the smartest men in the NHRA field. His son Kurt is also a successful pro stock driver.

Seasons: 1971–

National Event Wins: 96

NHRA Championships: 6 (pro stock: 1992, 1993, 1995, 1998, 1999, 2001)

Shirley Muldowney (born 1940)

Muldowney was the first woman to receive a drag racing license from the NHRA. For decades she has been a role model for female athletes around the world. But she didn't become famous just by being a woman in a male-dominated sport. She is also one of the greatest drag racers of all time, with three NHRA titles and 18 NHRA national event wins.

Seasons: 1965–2003

National Event Wins: 18

NHRA Championships: 3 (top fuel: 1977, 1980, 1982)

Warren Johnson's
pro stock car

Shirley Muldowney's
1980s-era top
fuel dragster

Don Prudhomme (born 1941)

The Snake earned his nickname with his lightning-quick reflexes. His legendary career began in top fuel. But he enjoyed his greatest success as a funny car driver. In 1975 he won the NHRA's first funny car points title, winning an amazing seven out of eight events. Along the way, Prudhomme became the most famous driver in drag racing. His success helped pave the way for the sport's spectacular growth. He finished his career where he started—in top fuel. He is now the owner of a successful NHRA team.

Seasons: 1962–1994
National Event Wins: 49
NHRA Championships: 4 (funny car: 1975–1978)

Angelle Sampey (born 1970)

The New Orleans, Louisiana, native is the winningest woman in NHRA history and is well on her way to becoming the winningest pro stock bike rider of all time. A former nurse, Sampey has ridden her U.S. Army–sponsored Suzuki to more than 40 event wins and three NHRA titles. She is ninth all-time among NHRA competitors in wins.

Seasons: 1996–
National Event Wins: 41
NHRA Championships: 3 (pro stock bike: 2000, 2001, 2002)

Don Prudhomme's 1970s U.S.
Army funny car

Angelle Sampey's U.S. Army
pro stock motorcycle

Gary Scelzi (born 1960)

In 2005 Scelzi beat out John Force for the NHRA funny car title. But Scelzi was a champion before he ever raced a funny car. In 1997 the Fresno, California, native became the first rookie to win an NHRA title in top fuel. He followed this up with two more top fuel titles in 1998 and 2000. He switched to funny cars in 2002 without missing a beat.

Seasons: 1997–

National Event Wins: 39

NHRA Championships: 4 (top fuel: 1997, 1998, 2000; funny car: 2005)

Tony Schumacher (born 1969)

In the 2000s, Schumacher has been the top fuel driver to beat. The Sarge and his U.S. Army–sponsored car have won the top fuel title four times—1999, 2004, 2005, and 2006. During that time, he has become one of the NHRA's biggest stars. He is the son of funny car legend Don Schumacher.

Seasons: 1996–

National Event Wins: 35

NHRA Championships: 4 (top fuel: 1999, 2004–2006)

Gary Scelzi's Mopar
Oakley funny car

Tony Schumacher's
U.S. Army top fuel
dragster

Glossary

aerodynamic: shaped so that air flows smoothly over and around an object

airfoil: a wing-shaped device that creates downforce

chassis: the main structure of a drag racing car. The other parts of the car are attached to the chassis.

combustion chamber: the part of an engine in which fuel and air ignite to create power

downforce: the force of air pushing down on a car as it moves forward

elapsed time: the period of time it takes a vehicle to get from the starting line to the finish line

fiberglass: a strong, durable material made of threads of woven glass

hood scoop: a slot of holes in a car's hood that allows extra air to reach the engine, creating extra power. Pro stock cars are equipped with hood scoops.

horsepower: a unit of measurement used to measure an engine's power

methanol: an alcohol-based fuel used in many drag racers

nitromethane: a powerful fuel for top fuel dragsters and funny cars

pit: an area near the track where the teams can rebuild and repair cars between runs

sponsors: companies that provide financial support for racing teams. Sponsors pay teams to advertise for them.

stock: straight from the factory

superchargers: devices that add horsepower to an engine by forcing air into the combustion chamber

suspension: the parts that connect the wheels to the main part of the car

Selected Bibliography

Genat, Robert. *American Drag Racing*. Saint Paul: MBI Publishing Company, 2001.

____. *Funny Cars*. Osceola, WI: MBI Publishing Company, 2000.

____. *Top Fuel Dragsters*. Saint Paul: MBI Publishing Company, 2002.

____. *Vintage and Historic Drag Racers*. Osceola, WI: MBI Publishing Company, 1998.

Post, Robert C. *High Performance: The Culture and Technology of Drag Racing, 1950–2000*. 2nd ed. Baltimore: Johns Hopkins University Press, 2001.

Reyes, Steve. *Quarter-Mile Chaos*. North Branch, MN: CarTech Books, 2006.

Further Reading

Doeden, Matt. *Stock Cars*. Minneapolis: Lerner Publications Company, 2007.

Piehl, Janet. *Indy Race Cars*. Minneapolis: Lerner Publications Company, 2007.

Raby, Philip. *Racing Cars*. Minneapolis: Lerner Publications Company, 1999.

Websites

John Force Racing
http://www.johnforceracing.com/
The legendary funny car driver's website features information about John Force, his daughter Ashley, and the rest of his championship-winning team.

National Hot Rod Association
http://nhra.com
The NHRA's website features race schedules and results, facts about teams and drivers, and lots of other useful information. For a list of its Top 50 drivers, visit http://www.nhra.com/50th/top50/list.html

Nitroactive.net
http://www.nitroactive.net
Check out the stunning photography of Nick Licata and others at this drag racing Internet site.

Index

About the Author

Jeffrey Zuehlke has written more than two dozen books for children, on subjects ranging from muscle cars to Poland to Henry Ford to Joseph Stalin. He lives in Saint Paul, Minnesota.

About the Consultant

Nick Licata is a drag racing photographer, magazine editor, and creator of www.nitroactive.net, a website dedicated to vintage and nostalgia drag racing, featuring memorabilia and photographs.

Photo Acknowledgments

The images in this book are used with the permission of: © Nitroactive.net, pp. 4-5, 6 (both), 7 (both), 20, 21, 22-23 (background), 23, 25, 26, 27, 28 (both), 29, 30, 31 (both), 32, 35 (bottom), 36 (top), 37 (top), 40 (top), 41 (top), 43 (bottom), 44 (both), 45 (both); © Jim Handy, pp. 8, 8-9 (background), 14, 38 (bottom); © Ralph Crane/Time & Life Pictures/Getty Images, p. 9; © Allan Grant/Time & Life Pictures/Getty Images, p. 10; © Mike Mueller, pp. 11, 12, 13, 17 (both), 18, 19, 35 (top), 36 (bottom), 37 (bottom), 39 (bottom), 41 (bottom), 43 (top); © Laura Westlund/Independent Picture Service, pp. 16 (left and bottom right), 33; © PhotoEquity/Artemis Images, p. 16 (top right); © Steve Reyes, pp. 34 (top), 39 (top), 40 (bottom), 42 (top); AP Photo/Auto Imagery, Inc., p. 34 (bottom); © Jon Asher, p. 38 (top); AP Photo/National Hot Rod Racing Association, p. 42 (bottom).

Cover: AP Photo/National Hotrod Racing Association